I0438443

THE MALE TEENAGER'S 9 LATE SIGNS OF ALCOHOLISM

*Becki Bateman,
with Dave Payne*

ALERT SERIES
(ACTUAL LEANING EXAMPLES TO RECOGNIZE TROUBLE)

Inspiring Voices®
A Service of **Guideposts**

Copyright © 2013 Becki Bateman, with Dave Payne.

All rights reserved. No part of this book may be used or reproduced by any means, graphic, electronic, or mechanical, including photocopying, recording, taping or by any information storage retrieval system without the written permission of the publisher except in the case of brief quotations embodied in critical articles and reviews.

Inspiring Voices books may be ordered through booksellers or by contacting:

Inspiring Voices
1663 Liberty Drive
Bloomington, IN 47403
www.inspiringvoices.com
1-(866) 697-5313

Because of the dynamic nature of the Internet, any web addresses or links contained in this book may have changed since publication and may no longer be valid. The views expressed in this work are solely those of the author and do not necessarily reflect the views of the publisher, and the publisher hereby disclaims any responsibility for them.

Any people depicted in stock imagery provided by Thinkstock are models, and such images are being used for illustrative purposes only.

Certain stock imagery © Thinkstock.

ISBN: 978-1-4624-0598-5 (sc)
ISBN: 978-1-4624-0597-8 (e)

Library of Congress Control Number: 2013907141

Printed in the United States of America.

Inspiring Voices rev. date: 04/24/2013

"*L ife is a Journey, not a destination.*" Inspiration, determination, and motivation has been inspired by so many wonderful people encountered on this marvelous adventure we call life. It would be impossible to name everyone responsible for helping me bring this dream to fruition. To Angie, Jenny, Carolyn, Mary Ellen, Mary, Charlie, Ann, Melinda, Melissa, my deepest gratitude!

Peggy, thank you for all the hours you have spent helping me edit this book.

I am most appreciative of the long-lasting love and friendship of L.M. who has been my personal muse throughout many years on this journey.

With deep pain (no pun intended, Dave) and heartfelt gratitude, this book and the other two in the series, are dedicated to Dave Payne, for his contribution to making this book a reality, for giving me the motivation to move the project "off the back burner and get cooking again," for his ability to balance the seriousness of a sobering subject with his wit and wisdom, and for providing the male perspective that was so invaluable for The Male Teenager's 9 Early, Middle, and Late Signs of Alcoholism. Certainly his scenarios were often more insightful from his viewpoint than mine.

Ironically, Dave was in hand-to-hand combat with his own disease the entire time we worked on this project. We had finished the first book of the three-part series and had begun writing the next two as ideas would come. Unfortunately, he passed away as the first book was moving into editorial review. Dave wanted to leave a lasting legacy. Hopefully his input into this series will be his greatest contribution, making a difference in a world that still does not understand how baffling, cunning, powerful, and insidious this disease truly is. He believed that young people need to recognize these early signs and become familiar with the available resources in order to get help earlier for this misunderstood malady.

Dave, thank you for your help. Your suggestions will continue to guide me and motivate me to complete the series in your memory.

BY THE SAME AUTHOR

ALERT (Actual Learning Examples to Recognize Trouble) Series:

Male Teenager's 9 Early Signs of Alcoholism
Male Teenager's 9 Middle Signs of Alcoholism
Male Teenager's 9 Late Signs of Alcoholism

Future publications:

Female Teenager's 9 Early Signs of Alcoholism
Female Teenager's 9 Middle Signs of Alcoholism
Female Teenager's 9 Late Signs of Alcoholism

HINTS (Helpful Information Needed To Succeed) Series

Congratulations! You have chosen the last of three in the ALERT (Actual Learning Examples of Recognizing Trouble) series centering on teenagers. After reading *The Male Teenager's 9 Late Signs of Alcoholism*, you should have a better idea how to recognize a young man's behavior that might indicate his disease has progressed through early-stage and middle-stage alcoholism into the final stage. At this stage, one has but four alternatives: mental-health facilities, hospitals, jails, or death! It can be noted that anywhere along the progression of this disease, one can choose the road to recovery. Your token can take you on this "subway train" all the way to the end of the line, but the earlier you get off the train, the better your chances of staying off. Also, if you haven't read the first two books of the series, you may want to read *The Male Teenager's 9 Early Signs of Alcoholism* and *The Male Teenager's 9 Middle Signs of Alcoholism* to increase your knowledge base of this disease.

Let's begin with some background information.

According to the National Institute of Health website one in ten drinkers in the United States becomes an alcoholic. That is approximately 17.6 million people. If that is the case and every alcoholic directly affects five to eight people, we are now looking at approximately 88 to 140.8 million Americans hurt by alcohol! These are the mothers, fathers, husbands, wives, children, close relatives, and friends of the alcoholic. Indirectly affected are the other friends, relatives, teachers, classmates, in-laws, coworkers, and acquaintances of the alcoholic; these people are not even considered in such numbers.

As you are reading, keep in mind that this series is not intended to be a collection of statistics or a rendering of research. With 232 million sites on the Internet alone and thousands of books at local libraries and bookshops, we suggest you gather other information as it relates to and interests you. Remember that statistics can vary depending on how they were collected and when they were found. Resources and web sites where you can gather more up-to-date information relevant to your journey are listed at the end of each book in the series. These same resources can assist you in learning how you might be of help to someone else.

In the '80's when the subject of alcoholism became popular on TV talk shows; in the movies; and in books on alcoholism, codependency, and adult children of alcoholics, there was an explosion of knowledge. Many of the books made it to the best-seller lists. At the same time drawing focus to these problems were national conferences such as these two: First Annual Conference on Alcoholism and the Family and Adult Children of Alcoholics. Unfortunately, over the next thirty years the attention diminished, but the problem has increased. A vast number of people still carry a stereotype of what a "typical" alcoholic looks and acts like.

If you are asked to close your eyes and picture an alcoholic, do you picture an old person panhandling for money on a street corner, a homeless person sleeping under a bridge or a piece of cardboard, or someone who is eating out of a dumpster? When you picture alcoholics, were any of them young? Were all of them male? Such images would not be entirely wrong; however, you would probably be picturing alcoholics in chronic or late-stage alcoholism, which is only 3 percent of the alcoholic population. No one wakes up in the chronic or late-stage of alcoholism; every drinker has had to go through the early and middle stages first.

Statistically, about 50 percent of alcoholics are male and 50 percent female. Younger and younger people are being treated for this affliction. Alcoholism does not discriminate. It will take any age, color, ethnic group, or occupation into its grip. For example, did you envision any alcoholic professionals such as doctors, nurses, teachers, lawyers, or clergymen? Name any occupation, and 10 percent are alcoholics in one of the three stages. They are referred to as "functioning alcoholics."

"Functioning" alcoholics are people who do not show any clear signs of having a problem. They perform well while on the job, are rarely absent, and often are cited for exemplary work. Some specific examples of those working in various professions and in one of the three stages of alcoholism are the following:

- A construction worker, who operates dangerous machinery and handles serious situations, but stops for a twelve-pack each day after work. He drives home well over the BAC (blood alcohol content).

- A priest who ministers to families; listens to confessions; conducts mass; visits shut-ins, the hospital patients, and prisoners routinely, yet he is a "weekend warrior." In other words, he drinks heavily on weekends consuming as much as someone else might drink throughout the entire week.
- A nurse whose job is to nurture and care for others hides alcohol during her workday in cupboards and cabinets. She does "maintenance drinking" throughout her day.
- A hotel manager whose main job is to run a smooth operation in servicing hundreds of guests throughout the week but comes in each day hung-over. He has to make excuses to go back to his office numerous times to take a drink from the bottle of booze locked inside his desk drawer.
- A corrections officer who is also the Employee Assistance Program (EAP) coordinator listens to coworkers, many with alcohol and drug problems, He sets them up with counseling, and refers them to a rehab or suggests a detox, yet he tries to deal with his own alcohol problem at home and at work.
- A medical doctor with a successful practice treats sick alcoholics and often does not recognize their affliction with alcoholism because she is in one of the stages and does not realize her alcohol problem either.
- A CEO who manages a major company on a daily basis, oversees a huge management team of professionals, interacts with other CEOs, but has martini luncheons and scotch-and-soda suppers. He does not see these as a potential problem with alcohol.

The list could go on and on as 10 percent of employees in *any* given occupation are alcoholic. Family, friends, and clients have absolutely no idea of their dependence on alcohol.

One of the most profound quotes from his movie "Chalk Talk on Alcoholism" was from Father Joseph Martin, who was well-known in the field of alcoholism. He stated, "By the time an alcoholic is in chronic stage alcoholism, any moron would know he's got a problem; that is only three percent of the alcoholic population. As a society, we need to be more informed about the 97 percent that are not in chronic alcoholism, but have the potential to be." He also stated, "If alcohol causes a problem, then it is a problem."

Many people in the 97 percent could be teenagers, yet this age group has not been adequately identified or addressed. Teens in general have a tougher time identifying with alcoholism. They can give many reasons why they're *not* alcoholics. They are too young; they haven't experienced loss of things, such as jobs, families, homes, or material things; they have not gotten kicked out of school, or been in jail, or prison, etc. They think, "They only party on the weekends like everyone else does" or "only have a couple" once in awhile. Teens do not recognize many of the signs of alcoholism.

If teens have not had a job to lose, have not started their own families, or have not acquired a significant amount of material things, they will not experience some of the losses that can indicate early drinking problems. Most teens do not want to do anything illegal or create problems to warrant getting arrested. If they do have any legal issues, they usually rely on their parents. Mom and Dad will sometimes deny that their kids have a problem. They may actually defend their son or daughter or bail him or her out of jail so their child does not suffer any consequences for this behavior.

Certain behaviors related to drinking have been recognized. There are nine signs in each of the three stages—(early, middle, and late)—for a total of twenty seven. These signs can help one to recognize how the disease progresses. How many teens would know any of them? More importantly, would they be able to cite specific examples in their own drinking problems that relate to these signs?

In reality each person is different, so the examples presented in this book—and the other two books in the series—could not possibly present all the ways and means a young person initially shows the symptoms of this disease. In 1956 the American Medical Association deemed alcoholism a disease. The reasons it was classified as a disease are the following:

1. There are four identifiable groups of people prone to the disease in our society: Children of Alcoholics, Native Americans, Teetotalers, and minority groups.
2. There are three stages—early, middle, and late—each with nine identifiable symptoms.
3. Alcoholism is progressive because it gets worse in each stage.
4. There is no cure, but the progression can be halted and it can be lived with by not taking the first drink.

Who are these groups in our society that are more prone to this disease? First are the children of alcoholics. These children are totally unaware that they are living in the midst of this malady.

They have no way of knowing that they have a 50 percent chance of becoming an alcoholic, marrying one, or both.

Second is the vast number of Native Americans. Many are still living on reservations.

Teetotalers are people who grow up in a home where everyone abstained from alcohol, so alcohol is a "forbidden fruit." As soon as these children leave the nest, some begin to drink heavily after their first encounter with this newfound "magic elixir." It is not what it does to them; it is what it does for them. They feel like they fit in. They can talk to guys or gals, ask them to dance or for a date, and, in general," have a great time"!

Progression of the disease shows how baffling, cunning, and powerful it truly is. The disease never gets better, only worse as it exhibits each one of the early, middle, and late signs. Alcoholism has an even stranger twist. Suppose someone has quit drinking for ten years and then begins again; the disease does *not* pick up where it left off ten years ago, but within a matter of time resumes as though the person had never stopped drinking for that length of time.

Remember, there is no cure, the progression can be halted and the disease lived with if one does not pick up that *first* drink!

We have already met J.D. in the first two books *The Male Teenager's 9 Early Signs of Alcoholism* and *The Male Teenager's 9 Middle Signs of Alcoholism*. He does not have a clue that he has passed through the first two stages of an alcoholic's progression and has crossed the thin line into late stage. The examples in this book will offer a variety of situations that will now show how

J.D. is exhibiting more behaviors in late stage. It is also hoped that as you read this you try to identify with each scenario instead of comparing. In other words, look for ways you are like the teen example, not how you are different. If you are reading this because you are concerned about a friend or relative who may be experiencing problems with alcohol, try to think of this person and how he or she would exhibit each one of the late signs and how you might be of help.

Keep in mind that every teen will progress at a different rate. He could remain in the early stage for ten to twenty years or for as little as a year or less. Many variables (e.g. the age he began drinking, his body chemistry, his height and weight, the amount he drinks, how often he drinks, what he drinks, what, if any, substances that he ingests into his body while drinking, etc) can affect the length of time in any stage.

It is not unusual for a teen to have started drinking before age thirteen. The younger a person is when he picks up the drink, the faster it affects him; his body, bones, and organs are still forming. A teen who weighs 95 pounds will progress through the stages faster than a young person weighing 140 lbs. or more. The five-foot-six-inch teen will also progress faster than the teen over six feet tall. A younger child drinking daily will show signs more quickly than a teen drinking a couple bottles of wine three or four times a week. If any other substances (drugs and/or pills, for example) are used while the young man is drinking, he will rapidly progress. Considering such factors, it is possible to go through the early stages of alcoholism in five years or less. If he begins using alcohol at thirteen he might enter the middle stage around eighteen, and he could be in the late stages of addiction in his early twenties! Again, each person's inner chemical makeup reacts differently to the alcohol and/or the substances he takes into his body. This also explains why we are seeing younger and younger kids ending up in hospitals, detox, rehabilitation centers, and other institutions.

When one is in each stage for a longer time then he could be considerably older in the final stage. This also can explain why an alcoholic is stereotypically pictured as someone older.

No one wakes up one morning and finds himself in late stage alcoholism. He has to progress through each of the three stages— early, middle, and late. There are physical, social, mental health, and legal risks woven into all stages.

Here's a quick overview of each stage and its symptoms:

The nine EARLY signs:

1. Hide it
2. Sneak/steal it
3. Angry when someone tries to talk to you about your drinking
4. Blame other people/places/things
5. Drink when something bad/good happens
6. Drink until supply is gone
7. Change in personality
8. Uncomfortable when not available
9. Blackouts

The nine MIDDLE signs:

1. Drink before a function
2. Loss of other interests
3. Preoccupation with drinking
4. Promises and Resolutions Fail Repeatedly
5. Neglect Personal Care-Hygiene/Food/Health
6. Problems with family, friends, work, school, money, etc.
7. Increased tolerance
8. Increased dependence
9. Blackouts—more frequent, longer in duration

The nine LATE signs:

1. Loss of family, friends, jobs
2. Loss of willpower (control)
3. Obsession with use
4. Physical and moral deterioration
5. Decrease in tolerance
6. Drinking with people beneath him or alone
7. Impaired thinking
8. Geographical cures
9. Mental health facilities, hospitals, jails, or DEATH

I n the first book of this series J.D., a typical 13-year-old teenager, was introduced. He got good grades in school, played sports, enjoyed the outdoors with the many activities that it offered, and had a wide circle of friends. His dad was a lab technician and his mom a social worker. His parents had never talked to him about drinking, but he knew his mother hated alcohol because she had lived with an alcoholic father and feared anyone when they drank. He also knew that his dad's mom had been an at-home drinker so his dad would not invite his friends to the house because he was afraid that his mom would embarrass him.

When J.D. turned 13 he had his first drink of alcohol. One of his friends challenged him to try it. Wanting to fit in with them, he drank that first one straight down. J.D. had never felt like he fit in at home or at school. With this first drink he was amazed by the effect it had on his mind and body. He never forgot how it gave him a warm feeling all over and a sudden rush to his brain; it made him feel like he mattered for the first time in his life. He continued to drink for a few more hours and the evening ended with his vomiting all over himself. Many, many times he vowed he would never drink like that again. But, of course, he did and his disease continued to progress without his being aware that denial plays a big part of it. (Alcoholism is the only disease known to humankind that the longer you have it, the more it convinces you that you *don't* have it!)

In the first book J.D. also exhibited all nine of the early warning signals that indicate trouble. Several of his behaviors became noticeable. He found ways and means to either hide or disguise the alcohol. He stole it from his parents' liquor cabinet and replaced the vodka or gin with water. In addition, he would get angry if anyone tried to talk to him about his drinking. Family members, friends, and some teachers bore the brunt of his anger. He started to drink if something good *or* bad happened. Vacations from school, his birthday, a friend's birthday, were all definitely reasons to celebrate. His grandfather's death, bad grades on a test, getting into trouble in a class, were times he drank when he was feeling sad. J.D. could not pass any bottle with some alcohol left in it; he would gulp it down not caring who had been drinking it.

Some other signs of the early stage of the disease were becoming apparent. J.D.'s personality began to change. When he drank no one ever knew if he would be funny and the life of the party, or if he would start an argument with someone regardless of size, age, or gender. Also, anywhere he went he had to make sure alcohol would be available or he would not want to go. Although not every alcoholic experiences blackouts, J.D. did have some. He thought everyone who drank had them; he also confused them with passing out. A blackout means a person can function but will not remember what he has done or only recall parts of it when he has sobered up. Passing out is getting so intoxicated that a person's brain and body literally shut down—on a floor, in the driveway, on a friend's living room floor, etc. He had experienced several blackouts in a six month period and could recall most of what he did.

In the second book of this series J.D. was in his mid-teens, continuing to drink, and subtly entered the next phase of his progression. During this time he lost another half dozen jobs. His excuses for losing the jobs were that he said his boss showed favoritism to other employees by giving them more hours and better work schedules. He dismissed the customers' complaints about him by calling them petty. He thought his coworkers were jealous. J.D. drank before he attended any kind of function. He found he relied on the booze to provide him with more ease and fun. All types of get-togethers such as sporting events, school dances, weekly card games with his buddies depended upon his having something to drink before he arrived.

More signs of his progression were shown when he lost interest in many of the activities and hobbies he enjoyed when he was younger. He lost all enthusiasm for the guitar and art lessons his parents had purchased. He dropped out of the after-school clubs he had eagerly joined. Instead of looking forward to these interests he wanted to spend his time hanging out with his new friends who liked to drink and party.

One of the biggest indicators at this stage was J.D.'s constant thinking about drinking. Alcohol was now choosing his friends, where he went, and what he did. He dropped out of school a few months after he turned seventeen having decided to quit before he got kicked out! In conversations his mind would drift off and he would often pretend to hear what people said. J.D. plotted and planned incessantly over grandiose ideas, plausible or not. He never thought about how to accomplish a single one.

J.D. made thousands of promises and resolutions to others and to himself. He promised he would go to his brother's game or his sister's dance recital. He would swear to his parents he would clean his room. He told his teachers he would turn in his homework on time. He told himself he would never drink that much again. The list goes on. After making such promises he never followed through.

J.D. was one who always prided himself on his appearance. Yet in this stage his clothing, hygiene, healthy eating habits, and physical fitness were no longer a priority. Many days he went without bathing. He would often wear the same clothes for several days.

His hair was unkempt most of the time. He would skip meals especially if he were drinking. He did not think about his health at all; he believed he was always "fine". People who had always cared about J.D. were now quite concerned about him.

Chaos, crisis, and calamities now surrounded J.D. His family threatened him with other living arrangements or nagged him to change how he was acting. The loss of many jobs did not faze him. He constantly got into trouble in school with teachers and classmates. Money posed a hardship as he never had enough. His drinking cost him more and more while at the same time his parents withdrew financial support. He borrowed money to pay back borrowed money; he had begun to run out of people to ask.

By this middle stage of alcoholism J.D. could drink a huge amount and prided himself that he did not show any obvious signs of intoxication. He would not slur his words, stagger when he walked, or stumble at all. He believed he could drink everyone under the table and was proud of it!

By now he depended more and more on the booze. He had vowed to himself he would *never* drink in the morning, but had begun to do exactly that. After a heavy night of drinking he believed alcohol calmed his nerves. He also found ways to get a needed drink throughout the day to help him cope. He had never thought he would drink morning, noon, and night.

J. D. still experienced blackouts, but now they were more frequent and longer in duration. At first they only happened every month or so, but in this second phase of alcoholism they occurred about every other week with significant gaps of memory loss. Can you "see" how J.D.'s experiences can be red flags to anyone familiar with the middle signs? J.D. is in serious trouble and does not have a clue.

Let us now take a look at each of the nine late signs of alcoholism and see how J.D. is handling them.

1. LOSSES: FAMILY, FRIENDS, JOB

FAMILY

J.D. has been drinking since he was 13 and in this time his addiction has put his family through a lot. His high school and the legal system labeled him with a PINS. This means he classifies as a Pupil In Need of Supervision. He skips school too many times, is difficult with several of his teachers, and is disruptive in the majority of his classes. While under the PINS he perpetually breaks many of the guidelines or rules. Eventually at 17 1/2 he is placed in a foster home, but he only lasts several months there. He does not follow the family's guidelines or curfew. Then he and another boy living there steal some cigarettes and liquor from the foster parents. These violations cause the courts to order him to a juvenile facility in another city where they would provide 24 hour supervision; he is no longer with his family.

FRIENDS

J.D. had been wasted for his last five birthdays. He vows this year will be different; he will not get drunk! He is really looking forward to this birthday. His friends are giving him a party at the beach. On his special day he gets so drunk that he passes out on the sand and wakes up in the morning to the sounds of seagulls. His head is pounding. He wonders what in the world happened! His friends have all deserted him and he feels so remorseful, shameful, and guilty. How could it happen again? Of course he says he will never drink like this again!

Early in his teenage years J.D. was very popular in school and involved in numerous activities. As time went on he began to lose touch with the friends he had known from elementary school; as his drinking increased these friends decreased. In a short time he hangs out with a totally different class of friends, but even they eventually turn their back on him so he feels abandoned and all alone.

JOBS

J.D. had two part-time jobs that he lost for lame excuses when he was fifteen and sixteen; he had worked at a neighborhood grocery store and then was hired at a fast food chain. Next he found jobs at a gas station, in a car repair shop, a restaurant, a discount store, a construction site, and a trucking warehouse. Now at nineteen he has already been fired from an electronics store and a pizza place where he was hired as a delivery boy. J.D. is quite shocked when he is fired once again from the convenience store where he has been employed for the past several months. His excuses were many; his coworkers were backstabbing him, his bosses were tyrants, the customers unappreciative; and the list could go on and on.

These are just some of the losses that a teen could have and use as excuses to continue drinking. How many more examples can you think of for this late sign?

2. Loss Of Willpower (Self-Control)

J.D. tells himself he will go out and just drink a couple cokes and then go home. After he downs them he convinces himself he can have just one beer. The next thing he knows he looks at the clock and six hours have passed. He has no idea how many drinks he consumed.

J.D. has lost count of the number of times he has said he will never drink again. When he began drinking at 13 he could stop after two or three drinks. He would get drunk only when he wanted to do so. As time progressed, the drinking became more of a problem in every area of his life—family, school, money, jobs, friends, etc. He cannot understand why he ends up getting wasted when he has only gone out to have a couple beers with his buddies.

J.D. now has a used car. He drives his car to the garage and is told it will take several hours to repair. Not wanting to sit around, he calls a friend who lives nearby. His friend picks him up and takes him back to his house. J.D. only intends to have one or two drinks and then pick up his vehicle. Four hours pass and J.D. realizes he is too drunk to get his vehicle or drive it home. His friend allows him to sleep it off on his couch. J.D. returns to the garage the next day using a ridiculous excuse for letting his car sit in the garage overnight. He is also dismayed when he is charged an extra fee for not picking it up on time.

What other examples have you seen when teens lose self-control or willpower over their drinking?

3. OBSESSION WITH DRINKING

B y now alcohol is clearly running not only J.D.'s life, but also is consuming his thoughts. It has made him push his old friends and family away. He cannot admit to himself how much he misses all of them especially his older brother and cute younger sister. Although he has talked to them on the phone, he has not seen them since he was placed in foster care at seventeen. Whenever he starts to think about them, it hurts too much. To numb the pain he switches his thoughts to his next drink. Now he begins descending into a history of mental health facilities, hospitalizations, and jails.

J.D. enjoys watching sports on TV and the commercials always get his attention. The majority of them are for some kind of alcohol. He finds himself curious about the taste and the effects of the various products. He continues to have these obsessive thoughts long after the games are over. Even though he has told himself that he really does not have the money for trying newer more expensive brands, nevertheless he would purchase them.

J.D. daydreams about drinking most of the time. In the morning he plans where and how he will drink. Throughout the day he engages in activities revolving around his drinking. In the evening he is already thinking about the following day. He worries he will not have enough money to buy it; afraid if someone were to see him buying so much; has anxieties about whether he will run out of booze. His fears multiply as his drinking increases.

While drinking J.D. dwells on all the "good times" he enjoyed with alcohol, and tries not to think what is presently going on in his life. Alcohol helps him fantasize about what he *will* do, the fun he *will* have with new friends, the great job he *will* get, the money he *will* earn, the women he *will* attract, the cars he *will* buy, the houses he *will* acquire, the clothes that *will* impress everyone, and on and on and on. These fantasies entertain a bright future; his current reality is the exact opposite.

Can you visualize how much of one's day can be consumed thinking about drinking? How many different examples can you name?

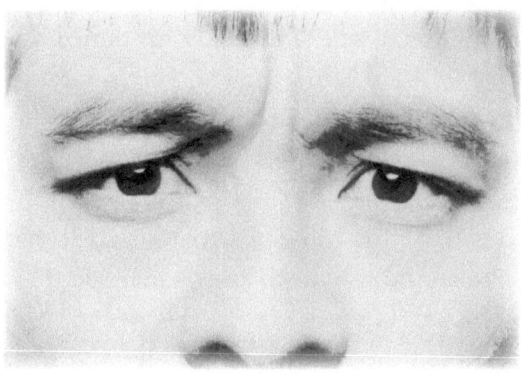

4. PERSONAL AND MORAL DETERIORATION

With his increased drinking J.D. at 19 is finding his energy levels are much lower than they used to be. Gradually he is sleeping more than usual, having difficulty getting up, and has a diminishing appetite. His physical appearance is changing; he has bags under his bloodshot eyes, his skin is beginning to look unhealthy, and his overall appearance is no longer a priority.

There was a time when J.D. believed that honesty was the best policy. Now he lies when it is just as easy to tell the truth. He started lying once in a while, but now his entire life is a lie. He lies to cover up lies! He is in denial and does not know it. There is an acronym for this: DENIAL (Don't Even "No" I Am Lying). He has told so many lies he believes them.

J.D. has had talks with his dad about sex. He had made the decision that he would wait until he was married. However at age 15 1/2 he lost his virginity to someone he met one night at a party. He quickly adopted the motto of "Lay 'em and Leave 'em." He is not interested in settling down and certainly could not picture himself with a family. Alcohol has convinced him he is having too much fun to do anything as dull as that.

These are just a few examples of the physical and moral deterioration that can happen as the disease progresses. Can you come up with a few different ones of your own?

5. Decrease In Tolerance

When J.D. began drinking at 13 it took just a few drinks to get a good buzz. In a little over a year it took a 12 pack to get the same feeling. Now at 19 he gets just as drunk on five or six beers, because his tolerance for the alcohol has decreased. These five or six beers have the same effect on him as the 12 or more did previously. J.D. used to be able to drink from mid afternoon to the wee hours of the morning. Gradually, he realizes he was getting drunk in less time with half or less of the amount.

It is now embarrassing to him how he can no longer "hold his liquor." He cannot believe how the booze causes him to say and do things he would never do before. He cannot control how he walks, talks, or reacts. J.D. sometimes staggers, stumbles, and slurs his words. He had told himself if he ever started to show these well-known signs of intoxication, he would stop drinking. Obviously the alcohol is in charge, not J.D.

J.D. tries to control the amount he drinks, but he notices a strange thing. Sometimes he can still drink a lot and other times he can have only a few drinks before he wonders what hit him! He tries to space his drinking, but to no avail. What is going on? Previously he believed he could predict how much he could drink and how it would affect him; now he is more confused by what is happening to him.

How many more examples for this late-stage symptom have you encountered?

6. Drinking With People Beneath Him

There is a saying that water seeks its own level. As a child J.D. had a great group of friends. He thought drinkers and druggies exhibited destructive behaviors. Slowly his elementary school friends were replaced with a rougher set of teens who seemed more exciting and adventuresome. Alcohol quickly dissolved these new friendships as well as his old ones. At 19 he has very few friends and spends a great deal of time alone. He believes no one cares.

J.D. used to hang out where all the kids his own age did. Now he goes to bars that cater to older people. He waits until most of them are quite wasted before he makes his appearance. He is well "lit" himself by the time he gets there, so he fits right in.

Even when there are no parties or no friend with whom to drink, J.D. still has an urge to go out drinking even if it means he will be alone in some strange place. He seeks out cheap "dives" with some strange characters. He finds a spot where he can drink and observe without being noticed. If anyone does approach him his body language tells them to get lost. He can kill hours in a place like this.

Can you name some other examples of how a teen can continue his downward spiral by seeking to drink with a rougher crowd?

7. IMPAIRED THINKING

J.D. has a doctor's appointment. On his way there he drives by his friend's house. Spotting his friend's car in the driveway, J.D. figures he has enough time to stop for just one beer and still make it to his appointment on time. He ends up staying and completely misses his appointment.

J.D. is partying with friends at the park. Joe who is highly intoxicated drives up on his new motorcycle. Joe dares J.D. to take it for a spin. Although J.D. has never driven a motorcycle before and has vowed he never would, he has had just enough alcohol to make him want to meet the challenge. He hops on the bike, roars away, and about 100 yards down the road takes a spill. He doesn't sustain any serious injury, but says he will never ride a motorcycle again! Within a week he is considering buying his own Harley. He does not have a job or any money saved for such a purchase, but he boasts to his friends he will own one by the end of the year.

Too many times to count J.D. is very intoxicated and thinks he is okay to drive. He gets behind the wheel and does not consider any consequences, especially the fact that it is illegal to drink and drive. Too often he will have others in the car with him and not care about their well being at all.

Can you cite other ways teenagers show impaired thinking while under the influence of alcohol?

8. GEOGRAPHICAL CURES

At fourteen and fifteen J.D. would sneak out of the house and go to a friend's where there would be booze. By the time he was sixteen, he decided to move into this friend's place where the beers flowed. After a couple months he moved back home, but the tension there could be cut with a knife. He knows he cannot stay there much longer.

Three years later his parents separate and he decides to live with his mom because his dad is moving to California. He does not want to leave his friends, but he changes his mind; his mother just does not understand him and keeps nagging him to get some help. Help for what? He knows his dad will be much easier to live with; besides they will be able to drink together. He lives with his dad until he is nineteen. He had already quit school, so he was free to go anywhere he wanted. Since he knew a guy in Florida the thought of going south seemed like a good idea. It wasn't long before J.D. and the "friend" part ways and he hears they are hiring in Texas. If that does not work out he can always head to Alaska and work on a fishing boat.

J.D. is restless, irritable, and discontent. He does not know what he wants to do with his life. He desperately wants to show the world what he is capable of accomplishing, but he does not know where to do this. One day he thinks about moving where no one knows him, getting his GED, and applying for college. His next thought is to move where construction is booming so he can get a great position and earn big bucks. He decides a couple of drinks will help him sort out his thoughts.

Can you think of other examples of how a teenage boy makes geographical changes based on alcohol's influence?

9. MENTAL HEALTH FACILITIES, HOSPITALS, JAILS, OR DEATH

As J.D. continues drinking he becomes depressed and has thoughts of suicide. He spends many hours consumed with thoughts of taking his own life. Alcohol seems to make these thoughts go away. He thinks he is going crazy! Then as the drinking continues his dad sends him back to his mom. J.D.'s mom gives him an ultimatum. She insists he call a Hot -Line number. He does that and is given an appointment at an alcohol referral center. There he is evaluated, kept as an in-patient for a week, and sent home with the suggestion to continue in an out-patient program. He attends the out-patient program for a few weeks, then starts being late or missing the weekly sessions. At nineteen he is constantly thinking of suicide and believes the only way out is to do it. After a failed attempt he is now committed to a mental institution for at least six weeks. When he is released from the mental health facility he is sober for a few days. He begins heavy drinking again. He finds himself attending a party where they are playing a dangerous game of beer pong to get drunk, but he drinks until he is unconsciousness. The kids panic, but one guy calls 911 and J.D. is taken to the hospital.

In the hospital J.D. is treated for alcohol poisoning and gets sent to their detox unit. From there he is transferred to a rehab for in-patient treatment. This is repeated three more times before he reaches the age of twenty-one. J.D. had one minor scrape with the law, but as the drinking continues he is stopped for a DUI and gets taken to the police station. His mother is called and she posts bail. He is warned that if he ever has another DUI he would be locked up. He promises that he will never drink or drive again. He is mandated to attend drug court, but only goes because he has to. When he completes this program, he returns to drinking heavily.

In this last stage of alcoholism he awakens in jail, remembering nothing. He does not know how he got there or what he had done. When he went before the judge the sentence was now an intense rehab and a half-way house after he completes the in-patient program. He would also have five years of probation. If he violates any of these orders he is reminded that he could land in prison.

The National Institute of Health has a list of some physical complications that can occur from drinking too much. A person can have withdrawal problems from alcohol such as alcohol ketoacidosis, liver disease, neuropathy, or delirium tremens. Alcohol ketoacidosis is most often seen in a malnourished person who drinks large amounts of alcohol each day. Liver damage may cause swelling and inflammation (hepatitis) in the liver. Over time this can cause scarring and then cirrhosis which is the final phase of liver disease. The cause of neuropathy is debated, but it probably includes both a direct poisoning of the nerve by the alcohol, and the effect of poor nutrition associated with alcoholism. Up to half of all long-term heavy alcohol users develop this condition. Delirium tremens can occur when you stop drinking after a period of heavy drinking, especially if one does not eat enough food. Doctors in every hospital warned J.D. that he might experience any of these conditions.

In this last stage of alcoholism what other events might occur?

B eing in late stage alcoholism J.D. has been in mental health facilities, hospitals, jail, and there is only one avenue left. The disease can dictate his death if he continues drinking, or he can ride the road of recovery. If you are reading this because you are concerned about your own drinking or someone else's, then the next few pages can begin to open up a wealth of resources for the help that is available. Now that you are more aware of the late signs of alcoholism, you may want to check out the previous two books in this series, *The Male Teenager's 9 Early Signs of Alcoholism and The Male Teenager's 9 Middle Signs of Alcoholism.*

Many young people fail to recognize any of these signs of alcoholism, but once you are aware of what to look for, you can see a potential problem and get help early. If you recognize two or more of these symptoms in one of your friends or even yourself as you read about J. D., ask for help. Remember, alcoholism is the only disease known to man that the longer you have this addiction, the more it convinces you that you don't!

Father Joseph Martin said, "If you had a friend or relative with cancer or another serious disease, wouldn't you get your hands on everything you could and read up on it to help them? I suggest you do the same thing with the disease of alcoholism." With that quote in mind, here are a few resources you can go to for further information:

Check the Yellow Pages for *Alcoholics Anonymous, alcoholism, treatment centers, Reach Out, rehabilitation services,* or, in the government offices section, found in front of phone book, see the listing under "county" for *alcohol/substance abuse services* or *chemical dependency services* or the listing under "state" for the health care hotline. Your local hospitals can also provide more information.

If you have never attended a self-help meeting or group, try to go to at least a dozen meetings to get a feel for which group you can best relate. Unfortunately, many people have preconceived notions about these groups that are not always true. Go to a meeting telling yourself you will learn at least one thing; if you identify with anyone or with any topic discussed, consider attending that group again; if you think you did not learn anything, go to another meeting in your area. Try not to convince yourself that some of the suggestions won't work for you before you try any. There are over a hundred self-help groups that can further your understanding. The following are some of the most widely known for alcoholism:

Alanon—The only requirement for membership is that there is a problem with alcohol in a relative or friend.

Alateen—The only requirement for membership is that there be a problem with alcohol in a relative or friend.

Alcoholics Anonymous—The only requirement for membership is a desire to stop drinking.

Children of Alcoholics or Adult Children of Alcoholics—These two programs are for men and women who grew up in alcoholic or other dysfunctional homes.

Co-Dependents Anonymous—The only requirement for membership is a desire for healthy and loving relationships.

Families Anonymous—This is a program of families and friends who have known a feeling of desperation concerning the destructive behavior of someone very near to them whether caused by drugs, alcohol, or other related behaviors.

Numerous prominent people have made significant contributions in the field of alcoholism and addiction. An Internet search and a review of their Wikipedia pages will help you find valuable information. The following people living or deceased have left a lasting legacy in the field of writing, teaching, training, speaking, or conducting workshops and seminars:

Melody Beattie—best known for her books *Codependent No More: How to Stop Controlling Others, Beyond Codependency and Getting Better All the Time, The Language of Letting Go, and Start Caring for Yourself* (www.melodybeattie.com)

Claudia Black—best known for her book *"It Will Never Happen to Me" Children of Alcoholics: As Youngsters-Adolescents-Adults* (www.claudiablack.com)

John Bradshaw—hosted numerous programs on PBS based on his books (www.johnbradshaw.com)

Betty Ford—the outspoken First Lady who founded Betty Ford Treatment Center

Ernie Larsen -best known for his Stage II Recovery process

John Lee—best known for his book *The Flying Boy: Healing the Wounded Man* (www.johnleebooks.com)

Marty Mann—the "First Lady of Alcoholics Anonymous," who went on to found the National Council on Alcoholism

Father Joseph Martin—a Roman Catholic priest, recovered alcoholic, and renowned speaker known for his video, *Chalk Talk on Alcoholism* and numerous other publications.

M. Scott Peck—the author of *The Road Less Traveled* and fourteen other books

Dr. Robert Smith—cofounder of Alcoholics Anonymous

Robert Subby—best known for his book *Lost in the Shuffle*

Sharon Wegscheider-Cruse—best known for her book *Another Chance: Hope and Health for the Alcoholic Family* (www.sharonwcruse.com

Bill Wilson—cofounder of Alcoholics Anonymous

Janet Woititz—know for her extensive work concerning adult children of alcoholics

Miscellaneous resources:

National Institute on Alcohol Abuse and Alcoholism
5635 Fisher Lane MSC 9304
Bethesda, MD 20892-9304
1-301-443-3860 www.niaaa.nih.gov/
www.nlm.nih.gov/medlineplus

If you do an Internet search for "films about alcohol and alcoholism," you will be given the names of some classic ones, such as *The Lost Weekend, Days of Wine and Roses,* and *Leaving Las Vegas.* Other films worth looking into include *My Name is Bill W.,* the story of Alcoholics Anonymous cofounder Bill Wilson, and *When Love Is Not Enough,* the story of Lois Wilson, founder of Alanon and wife of Bill Wilson both produced by Hallmark.

There are over 232,000,000 Web sites that result from a search just on "statistics for alcoholism," so you can see why it would be impossible to list them all. Here are some search terms to get you started:

Alcohol abuse
Current statistics on alcoholism
Adult alcohol abuse
Alcoholism
National statistics on alcoholism
Alcohol statistics by race
Alcohol-related deaths
Alcoholism family statistics
Statistics on alcohol in America
Alcohol consumption
Alcohol parent statistics

Of course, libraries are an excellent resource, as they have books, cassettes, magazines, books on tape, CDs, and DVDs on alcohol and alcoholism.

It is our sincere hope that this list of resources will enhance your journey to sobriety.

ABOUT THE AUTHOR

B ecki Bateman earned a BS and an MA in education in the 60's and early 70's. It was at the beginning of 1978 that she began her own personal recovery journey. The only reason she went to a meeting for anyone having a friend or relative with a drinking problem was to find an answer to get those people causing chaos, calamities, and crisis in her life to straighten up so she'd be okay! While attending those meetings she got to see videos, read books, and hear material on the family disease of alcoholism. One quote from Father Joseph Martin in one of his videos was "Never be impressed with people who hold degrees; after all rectal thermometers have them and you know where they put them."

In the early 80s, after taking courses in an alcohol and chemical dependency studies program at a local college, she was introduced to the early, middle, and late signs of the disease of alcoholism. This was the first time with all her education she not only realized what a stereotype she had of an alcoholic, but also recognized how angry she was at the educational system because it had not taught her about the one subject that had affected her life more than anything else. Around this same time she also began driving clients from a local rehab to another twelve-step program, where she heard others' stories. At first she compared herself, but slowly she started to identify when she heard them speak about their own experiences. She was a slow learner. After four and a half years of going to meetings to learn how to help others with their alcohol problems, she experienced a wake-up call. She realized she had a problem with alcohol and needed help.

Thus, her knowledge does not come from reading tons of books or paying thousands of dollars for classes; it comes primarily from being an active listener in a multitude of meetings in four different self-help programs, conferences, retreats, and workshops in a wide variety of places. She heard people share honestly of their pain, their denial, their experiences, their strength, and their hope. These experiences are the foundation of her journey that could have given her a PhD in the study of alcoholism. She became a student in the "University of Life".

Recognizing her own alcoholism was a major turning point in her life. Not only did it have a major impact on her personal life, but it enhanced her abilities as a teacher. She touched her students' lives in a way she never could have imagined. She could now recognize the "overachiever", "scapegoat", "lost child", and "mascot" in her classrooms. She incorporated some of her lessons around subject matter relating to alcohol or alcoholism. For example, she had sixth graders write about the three stages of alcoholism. Becki gained some of the children's trust so those who were living in a home with the three ground rules—don't ask, don't talk, and don't feel—could express themselves and reveal their feelings.

This journey has spanned over three decades, during which she attended numerous conferences and workshops. Some of the most significant were ACCEPT '81 (Atlantic City Conference on Education & Prevention Techniques). ACCEPT '83, and Annual Conferences on Alcoholism and the Family 1982-1986. In 1986, the conference changed its name to the Annual Conference on Chemical Dependency and the Family because the coordinators realized it didn't matter the substance or the behavior; the dynamics affecting the families living with any addiction were basically the same. In 1985, she went to California to attend TRIBES, a program which taught people how to work cooperatively in groups. She was the only person east of the Ohio River to be qualified as a trainer of trainers. In 1986, she attended the National Youth to Youth Conference in Ohio and the Family Restoration Workshop with Sharon Wegscheider-Cruise. In 1987, she went to the Third Annual Conference for Adult Children of Alcoholics. She was selected as an adult staff member for the Annual Youth to Youth Conferences in 1987-1989, where she quickly became known as "the warm fuzzy lady," and in August 1988, she was part of the First Annual Western Youth to Youth Conference in California. In November 1989 she participated in the Codependency & Intimate Relationship Conference in Florida.

In the early '90s, Becki and another coworker planned a Superintendent's Day on alcohol awareness. She remains active and the following article adds a little more to her accomplishments and illustrates how helping others allows her to pass on what she has been so freely given.

VOLUNTEER

Reprint of 1999 article)
Taken from the Hamilton Hall Herald, a newsletter of St.
Lawrence Alcoholism Treatment Center
December Issue 5

Variety is the spice of life, says an old adage. Until recently I
didn't realize the extent of volunteer work I had done throughout
my life.

Once upon a time I began my volunteering in a nursing home
during high school. It has continued to the present day in various
ways. During the growing-up years of my two daughters, I taught
Sunday school, eventually becoming Superintendent of Sunday
Schools.

Late in the 1970s, I became a volunteer at the St. Lawrence
Alcoholism Treatment Center. I drove patients to outside 12-
step meetings, made a rotating schedule coordinating seven
other volunteers, and got a dozen or more new recruits so more
meetings were available to the clients at the rehab.

Understanding more and more about addiction from attending numerous national conferences, workshops, retreats, I began a community prevention program called AIM AHEAD (An Involvement of Many—Awareness and Helping in the Education of Alcohol and other Drugs). Another important accomplishment was writing a weekly column in the At Your Leisure section of the local Sunday paper. The articles were all related to addiction and ran about five years.

Next, I began to share this information using another format. I made presentations and did trainings. One presentation was Expanding Our Horizons in Prevention at the 1986 NYFAC (New York Federation of Alcoholism Counselors) Conference. I also trained the local treatment center staff on Communication and Listening Skills for STAFF (Strategies and Techniques Affecting a Facility's Fellowship).

Then I served on different committees and boards. St Lawrence County was the largest county in New York State and the only one without a council. Serving on the original committee to establish a council for alcoholism, I was elected in 1986 to be on the first Board of Directors of the Alcohol and Substance Abuse Council of St. Lawrence County and was honored to be its president for two years. In addition I was asked to serve on the board of the North Country Freedom Homes, the Advisory Committee to the Mater Dei College Alcohol and Chemical Dependency Program, and also on the Community Advisory Board at the local treatment center.

Energetic, eager, earnest, teens kept me young at heart from 1985-1996 while working with Youth to Youth and YES (Youth Educating Society). A weekend every month or so found me, aka The Warm Fuzzy Lady" at a Youth to Youth conference in a high school in and around my county in New York State. The highlight was going to Russia and Ireland with a group of 50 teens and staff for a couple weeks in 1992 and with another similar group to Australia in 1995.

Every Thursday night from 1992-1999, I taught a recovery workshop at the local treatment center. "I've found GOD" (Good Orderly Direction), "I am not NUTS" (Not Using the Steps), and "I use TOOLS" (Techniques Offering Options with Love and Support) were just a few of the topics shared. Another project undertaken at this local treatment center was to gather recovery materials for the facility's library.

Recognized with awards such as volunteer of the year at the treatment center for 1994 and 1995 was a great honor. Then in 1999 I was awarded the volunteer of the year for the Northern Tier Providers Association of Alcohol and Substance Abuse Services. (Given to an individual who has given of their time and talent to provide assistance to the client community, promote community treatment and/or prevention efforts or advocate on behalf of those in need.) Years ago, I was promised that I was "going to go places, meet people, and do things I never dreamed possible." A couple years after that it was promised that I was "going to go places, meet people and do things I never dreamed possible **beyond my wildest dreams**. These volunteer experiences played a big part in fulfilling those promises.

NOTES

NOTES

www.ingramcontent.com/pod-product-compliance
Lightning Source LLC
Chambersburg PA
CBHW031328290526
45784CB00014B/2436

9 7 8 1 4 6 2 4 0 5 9 8 5